McGRAW-HILL

SCIENCE

Macmillan/McGraw-Hill Edition

Teacher's Edition

Richard Moyer • Lucy Daniel • Jay Hackett

H. Prentice Baptiste • Pamela Stryker • JoAnne Vasquez

NATIONAL GEOGRAPHIC SOCIETY

On the Cover:

The Siberian, or Amur, tiger lives primarily in the forests of eastern Russia. Some are also found in China and northern North Korea. Only about 400 of these beautiful animals still exist in the wild. About 500 captive Siberian tigers are in wildlife conservation programs. The survival of Siberian tigers in the wild depends on preserving their habitat and protecting them from poachers.

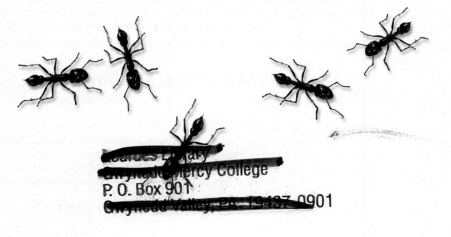

Macmillan McGraw-Hill

New York   Farmington

PROGRAM AUTHORS

Dr. Lucy H. Daniel
Teacher, Consultant
Rutherford County Schools,
North Carolina

Dr. Jay Hackett
Professor Emeritus of Earth Sciences
University of Northern Colorado

Dr. Richard H. Moyer
Professor of Science Education
University of Michigan-Dearborn

Dr. H. Prentice Baptiste
Professor of Science and Multicultural Education
New Mexico State University
Las Cruces, New Mexico

Pamela Stryker, M.Ed.
Elementary Educator and Science Consultant
Eanes Independent School District
Austin, Texas

Dr. JoAnne Vasquez
Elementary Science Education Consultant
Mesa Public Schools, Arizona
NSTA Past President

NATIONAL
GEOGRAPHIC
SOCIETY
Washington, D.C

The features in this textbook entitled "Invitation to Science," "Amazing Stories," and "People in Science," as well as the unit openers, were developed in collaboration with the National Geographic Society's School Publishing Division. Copyright © 2002 National Geographic Society. All rights reserved.

The name "National Geographic" and the Yellow Border are registered trademarks of the National Geographic Society.

Macmillan/McGraw-Hill

*A Division of The **McGraw·Hill** Companies*

Published by Macmillan/McGraw-Hill, of McGraw-Hill Education, a division of The McGraw-Hill Companies, Inc., Two Penn Plaza, New York, New York 10121. Copyright © 2002 by Macmillan/McGraw-Hill. All rights reserved. No part of this publication may be reproduced or distributed in any form or by any means, or stored in a database or retrieval system, without the prior written consent of The McGraw-Hill Companies, Inc., including, but not limited to, network storage or transmission, or broadcast for distance learning.

Printed in the United States of America

3 4 5 6 7 8 9 073/046 07 06 05 04 03 02

McGRAW-HILL
science
Macmillan/McGraw-Hill Edition
TEACHER'S EDITION

Table of Contents

Kindergarten	Grade 1	Grade 2	Grade 3

LIFE SCIENCE

Kindergarten

Unit 2 - *Learn About Plants*
1 Living Things
2 Parts of Plants
3 Plants with Flowers
4 Seeds, Seeds, Seeds
5 How Plants Grow
6 Plants We Use

Unit 3 - *Learn About Animals*
1 Our Pets
2 Animals that Fly
3 Animals that Swim
4 Animals that Walk
5 Animal Babies
6 People and Animals

Grade 1

Unit A - *Plants Are Living Things*
1 Your Senses
2 Living and Nonliving Things
3 Plants Are Living Things
4 Plants Have Parts
5 Roots
6 Stems and Leaves
7 Seeds
8 Plants Grow and Change

Unit B - *Animals Are Living Things*
1 Animals Are Living Things
2 Mammals
3 More Animal Groups
4 Grow and Change
5 Getting Food
6 Where Animals Live
7 Staying Safe

Grade 2

Unit A - *Plants and Animals*
1 Plants Are Living Things
2 Parts of Plants
3 Plants Make New Plants
4 Everyone Needs Plants
5 All Kinds of Animals
6 Animals Meet Their Needs
7 Animals Grow and Change

Unit B - *Homes for Plants and Animals*
1 Where Plants and Animals Live
2 Life in a Woodland Forest
3 Life in a Rain Forest
4 Life in a Desert
5 Life in the Arctic
6 Life in a Fresh Water Habitat
7 Life in a Salt Water Habitat
8 Caring for Earth's Habitats

Grade 3

Unit A - *Looking at Plants and Animals*
1 How Living Things Are Alike
2 The Needs of Plants
3 The Life Cycle of a Plant
4 The Needs of Animals
5 How Animals Grow
6 Parts of Animals
7 Kinds of Animals

Unit B - *Where Plants and Animals Live*
1 Ecosystems
2 Food Chains and Food Webs
3 Roles for Plants and Animals
4 Competition Among Living Things
5 Adaptations for Survival
6 Changing Ecosystems

EARTH SCIENCE

Kindergarten

Unit 4 - *A Home Called Earth*
1 Look Around You (landforms)
2 Rocks Everywhere
3 The Soil Under Your Feet
4 Water All Around
5 What Living Things Get from Earth
6 Take Care of Earth

Unit 5 - *Weather and Seasons*
1 All Kinds of Weather
2 Hot and Cold
3 The Sun
4 The Wind
5 Watch the Weather
6 The Seasons

Grade 1

Unit C - *The Sky and Weather*
1 The Sun
2 The Moon and Stars
3 The Planets
4 Weather
5 Weather Changes
6 Spring and Summer
7 Fall and Winter

Unit D - *Caring for Earth*
1 Rocks and Minerals
2 Soil
3 Water
4 Air
5 Living Things Are Resources
6 Pollution
7 Caring for Earth's Resources

Grade 2

Unit C - *Changes on Earth*
1 Water and Our Weather
2 Earth Can Change Slowly
3 Earth Can Change Quickly
4 Clues in Rocks
5 Putting the Clues Together
6 Life on Earth Changes

Unit D - *The Sun and Its Family*
1 Day and Night
2 Seasons
3 The Moon
4 The Moon Changes
5 Stars
6 Planets

Grade 3

Unit C - *Our Earth*
1 Minerals and Rocks
2 Kinds of Soils
3 Fossils and Fuels
4 Water in Sea, Land, and Sky
5 Saving Our Resources
6 Landforms
7 Slow Changes on Land
8 Fast Changes on Land

Unit D - *Cycles on Earth and in Space*
1 The Weather
2 The Water Cycle
3 Describing Weather
4 How Earth Moves
5 Phases of the Moon
6 The Sun and Its Planets

PHYSICAL SCIENCE

Kindergarten

Unit 1 - *Learn About Your World*
1 Use Your Eyes
2 Use Your Ears
3 Smell, Touch, and Taste
4 Tell About It
5 Same or Different
6 Make Groups

Unit 6 - *Make Things Move*
1 Move Along
2 Push and Pull
3 Slide and Roll
4 Wheels
5 Magnets
6 Float or Sink

Grade 1

Unit E - *Matter, Matter Everywhere*
1 Properties of Matter
2 Solids
3 Liquids
4 Gases
5 Solids in Mixtures
6 Solids and Liquids in Water
7 Heat Changes Matter

Unit F - *On the Move*
1 Things Move
2 Measure Movement
3 The Ways Things Move
4 Things Magnets Move
5 A Magnet's Poles
6 Things Magnets Pull Through
7 Moving Things Make Sound
8 Explore Different Sounds

Grade 2

Unit E - *Matter and Energy*
1 Matter All Around
2 Three States of Matter
3 Changing Matter
4 Heat
5 Light
6 Sound

Unit F - *Watch It Move*
1 Pushes and Pulls
2 Forces and Change
3 Levers
4 Ramps
5 All About Magnets
6 Everyday Magnets

Grade 3

Unit E - *Forces and Motion*
1 Motion and Speed
2 Forces
3 Changes in Motion
4 Doing Work
5 Levers and Pulleys
6 More Simple Machines

Unit F - *Looking at Matter and Energy*
1 Properties of Matter
2 Comparing Solids, Liquids, and Gases
3 Building Blocks of Matters
4 How Heat Travels
5 How Light Travels
6 Properties of Sound
7 Paths for Electricity

Grade 4

LIFE SCIENCE

Unit A - *The World of Living Things*
1 The Cells in Living Things
2 Classifying Organisms
3 Organisms of the Past
4 Organisms and Where They Live
5 Changes in Ecosystems
6 Plant Parts
7 Plant Growth and Reproduction

Unit B - *Animals as Living Things*
1 Animal Characteristics
2 Animals Without Backbones
3 Animals with Backbones
4 Organ Systems
5 Development and Reproduction
6 Animal Survival

EARTH SCIENCE

Unit C - *Earth and Beyond*
1 What You Can Learn from Rocks
2 Clues from Fossils
3 Shaping Earth's Surface
4 The Story of Soil
5 Inside Earth
6 Earth, the Moon, and the Sun
7 The Solar System and Beyond

Unit D - *Water and Weather*
1 Water, Water Everywhere
2 Follow the Water (water cycle)
3 Motions in the Oceans
4 Go with the Flow (groundwater)
5 Water Please! (conservation)
6 Air, Wind, and the Atmosphere
7 Weather and Climate

PHYSICAL SCIENCE

Unit E - *Matter*
1 Matter (properties, states)
2 Measuring Matter
3 What Matter Is Made Of
4 Physical Changes
5 Chemical Changes

Unit F - *Energy*
1 Motion, Forces, and Energy
2 Energy and Tools
3 Heat
4 Light
5 Sound
6 Static Electricity
7 Current Electricity
8 Electricity and Magnetism

Grade 5

Unit A - *Structures of Plants and Animals*
1 Classifying Living Things
2 Roots, Stems, and Leaves
3 The Importance of Plants (photosynthesis)
4 Plants Without Seeds
5 Plants with Seeds
6 Flowers and Seeds
7 Plant Responses and Adaptations
8 Animal Structure and Function
9 Animal Adaptation

Unit B - *Interactions of Living Things*
1 Living Things and Their Environment
2 Food Chains and Food Webs
3 Cycles of Life
4 How Populations Survive
5 Biomes
6 How Ecosystems Change

Unit C - *Earth and Its Resources*
1 Earth and Its Neighbors
2 Earth's Changing Crust
3 Minerals of Earth's Crust
4 Earth's Rocks and Soil
5 Earth's Atmosphere
6 Earth's Fresh Water
7 Earth's Oceans
8 Energy Resources

Unit D - *Weather and Climate*
1 Atmosphere and Air Temperature
2 Water Vapor and Humidity
3 Clouds and Precipitation
4 Air Pressure and Wind
5 Air Masses and Fronts
6 Severe Storms
7 Climate

Unit E - *Properties of Matter and Energy*
1 Physical Properties
2 Elements and Compounds
3 Solids, Liquids, and Gases
4 Mixtures and Solutions
5 Chemical Changes
6 Acids and Bases
7 How Matter and Energy Interact

Unit F - *Motion and Energy*
1 Newton's First Law
2 Newton's Second and Third Laws
3 Newton's Law of Gravitation
4 Sound Waves
5 Pitch and Loudness
6 Reflection and Absorption
7 Light and Mirrors
8 Light and Lenses
9 Light and Color
10 Invisible Light

Grade 6

Unit A - *Classifying Living Things*
1 The Kingdoms of Life
2 Classifying Plants
3 Invertebrates
4 Vertebrates
5 Reproduction and Growth

Unit B - *Organization of Living Things*
1 From Cells to Ecosystems
2 Comparing Earth's Biomes
3 Parts of a Cell
4 Movement and Nutrition in Cells
5 Cells Divide and Grow
6 The History of Genetics
7 Predicting Traits
8 How DNA Controls Traits
9 Using Genetics

Unit C - *Observing the Sky*
1 The Tools of Astronomers
2 Earth and the Sun
3 The Moon in Motion
4 The Inner Solar System
5 The Outer Solar System
6 Stars
7 Galaxies and Beyond

Unit D - *The Restless Earth*
1 Moving Plates
2 Earthquakes
3 Volcanoes
4 Making Mountains and Soil
5 Erosion and Deposition
6 The Rock Cycle
7 Geologic Time

Unit E - *Interactions of Matter and Energy*
1 Physical Properties of Matter
2 Elements and Atoms
3 Chemical Changes
4 Temperature and Heat
5 How Heat Affects Matter
6 Sources of Energy
7 Static Electricity
8 Circuits
9 Electromagnets
10 Using Electricity

Unit F - *Motion, Work, and Machines*
1 Speed and Distance
2 Forces and Motion
3 Acceleration and Momentum
4 Energy and Work
5 How Levers Work
6 How Inclined Planes Work

Meeting National Science Standards

National Science Education Standards

The National Research Council set up a
National Committee on Science Education Standards and Assessment
to develop national standards in science education.
The Standards are summarized in these categories:

- Science as Inquiry
- Physical Science Content
- Life Science Content
- Earth and Space Science Content
- Science and Technology
- Science in Personal and Social Perspectives
- Nature and History of Science
- Unifying Concepts and Processes
- Fair, Consistent Assessment in a Variety of Contexts

Benchmarks for Science Literacy

The groundbreaking Project 2061 as presented in a report of the
American Association for the Advancement of Science,
the Benchmarks for Science Literacy,
provides teachers with common goals without requiring
uniform curricula and methods.

The Benchmarks can be summarized by:

- The Nature of Science
- The Nature of Technology
- The Physical Setting
- The Living Environment
- The Human Organism
- Common Themes

McGraw-Hill Science was developed to enable teachers to implement
these national science standards within the context of their
own state and local science criteria by focusing on three major aspects:

- **the tools and processes of inquiry in every lesson**
- **grade-level sequenced content**
  with life, earth, and physical sciences
  taught at each grade
- **assessment in a variety of contexts**

Pages TR2–TR3 in the Teacher Reference Section present a
correlation of the units of this grade level to both sets of these national standards.

Assessment in *McGraw-Hill Science*

McGraw-Hill Science provides a variety of contexts for assessment while students are learning and at ends of lessons, chapters, and units.

The assessment is student-centered, encompassing a four-fold assessment plan:

? Ongoing Assessment	**Pupil Edition** This logo on the pages of the Pupil Edition earmarks a question that students can answer before turning the page, allowing for self-assessment and an opportunity to reread and review before going on.
✓ Informal Assessment	**Teacher Edition** On the last page of each lesson, the Teacher Edition provides activity-oriented, informal assessment strategies that are leveled easy/average and challenge.
✓ Formal Assessment	**Pupil Edition** ▪ Lesson Reviews (Think and Write) ▪ Chapter Review and Test Prep **Reading in Science Resources** ▪ Lesson Vocabulary Review and Cloze Tests ▪ Chapter Vocabulary Review ▪ Unit Vocabulary Review **Assessment Book** ▪ Chapter Tests Formal written assessment is provided for each lesson and chapter in the Pupil Edition and with the **Reading in Science Resources** blackline masters. Chapter Tests are provided in the separate **Assessment Book** blackline masters.
Performance Assessment	**Pupil Edition** ▪ Explore Activities: Going Further ▪ Unit Performance Assessment **Assessment Book** ▪ Unit Performance Assessment Students are given many opportunities to think through problems and show what they can do. Each Explore Activity provides a Going Further step that invites them to inquire further. Each unit has multiple Performance Assessment tasks.

Portfolio Assessment

McGraw-Hill Science provides blackline masters *(Activity Resources)*
to accompany all activities in the Pupil Editions,
and Chapter Graphic Organizers *(Reading in Science Resources)*
as well as *School to Home Activities* and *Cross Curricular Projects* blackline masters
from which students can select items to build a portfolio.

Building Science Process Skills in McGraw-Hill Science

Building the skills of inquiry empowers students to solve problems, to evaluate their solutions, and to plan and implement their own investigations.

McGraw-Hill Science **has a three-fold plan for building science process skills:**

Introduction

Invitation to Science
Pupil Editions open with skill instruction in the real-life context of a working scientist.

Skill Instruction

Process Skill Builders
Special activities teach students how to use a process skill to accomplish a task.

Consistent Practice

Explore Activities Quick Labs
When students use a process skill in an activity, the step is labeled and highlighted.

The Process Skills taught in *McGraw-Hill Science Grades 3 to 6* are:

Observe	To use one or more of the senses to identify or learn about an object or event
Infer	To form an idea from facts or observations
Classify	To place things that share properties together in groups
Measure	To find the size, distance, time, volume, area, mass, weight, or temperature of an object or event
Use numbers	To order, count, add, subtract, multiply, and divide to explain data
Communicate	To share information
Predict	To state possible results of an event or experiment
Interpret data	To use the information that has been gathered to answer questions or solve a problem
Form a hypothesis	To make a statement that can be tested to answer a question
Use variables	To identify and separate things in an experiment that can be changed or controlled
Experiment	To perform a test to support or disprove a hypothesis
Make a model	To make something to represent an object or event
Define based on observations	To put together a description that is based on observations and experience

Developing Reading Skills in McGraw-Hill Science

Before– and After–Reading Questions

- **Before Reading**
  All Pupil Edition headings are questions that students can try to answer before reading.

- **After Reading**
  A corresponding question is provided at the end of each page or two-page spread to allow students to assess their comprehension.

Developing Vocabulary

- **Preview**
  The Teacher Edition provides a Chapter Vocabulary Preview on each Chapter Opener spread. The Pupil Edition previews vocabulary on the opening spread of each lesson.

- **Point of Instruction**
  Each vocabulary word is highlighted in yellow at the point where it is taught. At point of appearance the side column of the Teacher Edition provides a vocabulary teaching strategy for each vocabulary word.

Reading MiniLesson

Throughout the lessons, the Teacher Edition provides Reading Skill MiniLessons. Each MiniLesson is a brief tutorial and an activity for students to practice a specific reading skill for each chapter. One of the following skills is developed in each chapter:

- **Compare and Contrast**
- **Find the Main Idea**
- **Cause and Effect**
- **Draw Conclusions**
- **Sequence of Events**
- **Summarize**

Reading Strategy

The Teacher Edition provides additional opportunities for students to develop and apply reading skills. A listing on each Chapter Opener shows where the following skills are taught.

- **Cause and Effect**
- **Compare and Contrast**
- **Draw Conclusions**
- **Find the Main Idea**
- **Sequence of Events**
- **Summarize**
- **Ask Questions**
- **Reread**
- **Retell (paraphrase)**
- **Interpret Graphic Sources of Information**
- **Build on Prior Knowledge**
- **Organize Information**

Reading in Science Resources

Throughout the Teacher Edition, reductions of blackline masters for:
- Lesson Outlines
- Interpret Illustrations

from the *Reading in Science Resources* are provided at point of use.

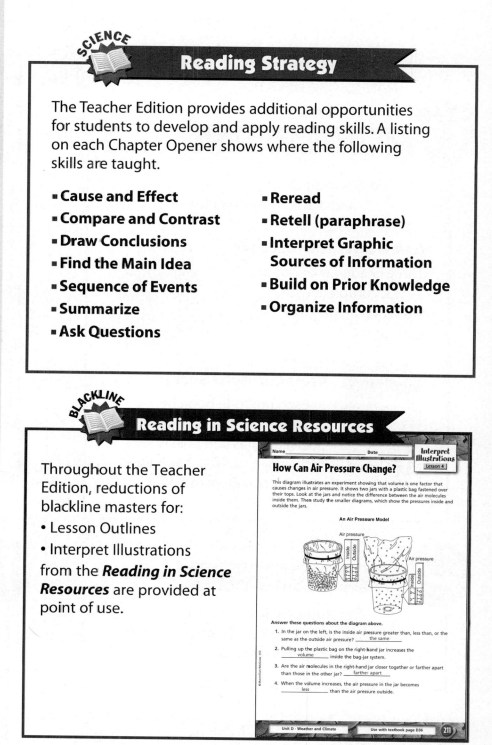

L·I·N·K·S

to Reading, Writing, Arithmetic, and More

McGraw-Hill Science is linked to all parts of your daily curriculum.

Students can integrate what they learn in science with what they learn throughout the day.

L·I·N·K·S

LESSON LINKS

At the end of each lesson students will find a Links column:

You will find Links to:

LITERATURE LINK

Additional outside reading for science and across the curriculum

Grade-Level Science Books

Three Grade-Level Science Books, complete with student activities, for each unit.

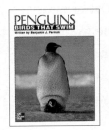

Cross Curricular Books

In each unit one book per chapter from the Reading and Social Studies curricula is pictured in the Teacher Edition at point of suggested use.

MATH LINK

The student will find activities involving graphs, measurements, problem solving, and shapes.

SOCIAL STUDIES LINK

Students will find activities involving map skills, cultural perspectives, and more.

MUSIC/ART LINK

Students will find activities making drawings, posters, models, as well as composing songs. In addition, opportunities to draw and create models abound in Explore Activities and Unit Performance Assessments.

HEALTH LINK

Students will find activities involving growing and staying healthy.

WRITING LINK

Students will have opportunities to write paragraphs, poems, stories, and skits.

TECHNOLOGY LINK

Students can find
- links on the Internet
- research projects on the Internet
- opportunities to use the Science Newsroom CD-ROMs

CROSS CURRICULAR PROJECTS

This blackline master booklet provides cross curricular projects organized into easy to use activities for each unit, complete with a Unit Culminating Activity.

Materials

Consumable materials (based on six groups)

Materials	Quantity Needed per group	Kit Quantity	Unit/Lesson
Ammonia solution		100 mL	E/6
Animals, pill bugs or sow bugs	8	coupon for 50	A/9
Animals, bugs, sow; earthworms; snail (pond)	4, 2, 8	coupons for 12 of each	B/1
Animal, snail, helix	2	coupon for 18	B/1
Antacid		2 tablets	E/6
Bag, plastic sandwich	4	80	C/2, D/4, F/8
Bag, plastic zip lip, 6" x 8"	1	12	C/4
Bag, plastic zip lip, 4" x 6"	1	6	F/4
Bag, specimen	1	12	D/2
Baking powder		7 oz	E/5
Baking soda		454 g	E/5, 6
Balloon, round, 5"	1	35	E/1
Balloon, long, 18"	1	10	F/2
Batteries, D-cell	12	24	E/7; F/7, 8, 9
Battery, 1.5 V alkaline, D-cell	1	6	E/7
Bottle, plastic, with cap	1		E/3
Bulb, 100 W	3	6	B/3, D/1, E/3
Cards, index		100	F/8
Cardboard sheet	6		A/5
Cardboard strip, 12 cm long	12		C/5
Cardboard tubes, long	2		F/6
Carton, small milk	4		B/4
Chalk	1 stick	12	C/5
Clay (cream)		2 lb	C/1, D/1
Clay (red, blue, green, yellow)		4 lb	C/2
Conifer, small pine seedling, or other	1		A/5
Crayons			E/5, F/9
Cup, foam, 8 oz	1	25	C/3, 4; F/4
Cups, paper, 100 mL, 200 mL	6, 2	50, 25	E/5
Cup, paper, 360 mL	1	25	A/7
Cup, plastic clear, 9 oz		150	B/5; C/4, 5, 6; D/2,3; E/3, 4, 6; F/8, 9
Detergent, powdered			E/6
Filters, coffee	1	100	E/4
Fingernail polish, clear			A/5
Foil, aluminum, 12" x 25'		1 roll	A/3; E/1; F/8, 10
Food coloring, dark red, 30 mL		2 bottles	A/1; D/2, 3; F/8
Food coloring, red, yellow, blue and green, 8 mL/ea		2 pkg	C/6,7;F/9
Food, banana, graham cracker crumbs, hazelnut, peanut butter			C/2
Food, beverage, carbonated			E/6
Food, celery stalk, piece of moss, or edible leaves			A/1, A/2
Food, cornstarch		500 g	E/5
Food, juice, grape, orange			E/6
Food, juice, lemon		15 oz	E/6
Food, marshmallows, large and small			E/2
Food, sugar cube	3	96	E/4
Food, tea bag	1	24	C/6, E/6
Food, vinegar		500 mL	C/5; E/5, 6
Food, whipping cream			E/4
Gloves, disposable		50 pair	E/6

Materials	Quantity Needed per group	Kit Quantity	Unit/Lesson
Gravel/pebbles		3 kg	B/1
Hydrogen peroxide, 3%, 230 mL		1 bottle	B/5
Iodine solution		100 mL	E/5
Iron filings		8 oz	E/4
Knives, plastic	3	24	A/1; C/2, 5
Microscope cover slip	3	100	A/1, 4; B/5
Paper, black	2 sheets		D/1
Paper, graph			C/1, D/1 E/4, F/1
Paper, wax, 75 sq ft		1 roll	C/2, E/5, F/8
Pen, marking	1		A/7
Pencil, wax marking	1	3	A/7
Petroleum jelly		4 oz	C/5
pH paper, blue and red litmus test	9	100 each	E/6
pH paper, wide range		100	E/6
Plant, cactus	1		A/2
Plant; duckweed, Lemna minor		coupon for 1 class package	B/1
Plant, Elodea	2	coupon for 12 sprigs	A/1, 2; B/1
Plant, fern, not w/spore cases	2		A/1
Plant, fern, w/spore cases		1 coupon	A/4
Plant, flowers, several large, from different plants	1		A/1, 2, 5, 6
Plant, garden or house, such as geranium	1		A/5, 7; D/2
Plant, grass	1		A/5
Plant, ivy	1		A/7
Plant, moss	2		A/1, 4
Plant, window or aquarium	1		A/3
Plastic wrap, 50 sq ft		1 roll	B/1, C/5
Rubber bands, medium		100	C/5; D/3, 4
Rubber bands, short	1	1 oz	F/1
Rubber bands, 5", long	1	approx. 80	F/2, 4
Salt		1,474 g	C/7; E/4, 5
Salt, kosher		2 lb	C/3
Salt, rock		1 lb	C/3
Sand, fine		2.5 kg	B/5, C/4, E/4
Sandpaper, $8\frac{1}{2}$" x 11"	2 pieces	3 sheets	E/5, 7
Seeds, corn; lima bean		30 g; 2 oz	A/6
Seed, grass		60 g	A/7, B/1
Seeds, pinto bean	44	1 lb	A/7, B/4
Soil, clay		10 kg	B/3, D/7
Soil, potting		24 lb	A/7; B/1, 4, 5; C/4, 6
Sound maker (clicker or timer)	1		F/6
Spoons, plastic	10	24	B/5; C/3, 4; E/4, 5
Straws, plastic		200	F/2, 5, 10
Straws, wrapped		50	C/7
String		200 ft	throughout
Swabs, cotton		72	E/6
Toothpicks		3 boxes	A/4, 6; D/1; E/2, 4, 5
Vinegar		3 bottles	C/5

Materials

Non-consumable materials (based on six groups)

Materials	Quantity Needed per group	Kit Quantity	Unit/Lesson
Apron	5		E/6
Balance, double pan, w/masses	2	1	C/4, E/1
Ball, golf	2	6	E/1, F/3
Ball, table tennis	1	6	F/3
Battery holder w/ Fahnestock clips	2	6	E/7
Blocks, triangular; 30°, 60°, 90°	1 of each	6 of each	D/1
Books, research			B/6
Bottle, 1 qt	1		A/1
Bottle, 2-L plastic	2		D/6
Bottle, spray	1	6	D/7
Bowl, foam, 12 oz	1	25	D/1
Bowl, plastic, 40 oz	1	12	E/4
Bowl, squat, 8 oz	1	6	C/6
Box, sealed, opaque	3		E/2
Box, shoe	1		E/1
Box, small cardboard with lid	1		F/7
Calculator	2		B/4, C/4
Camera (optional)	2		A/7, B/2
Can, empty	1		B/3
Car, toy	1	6	F/2
Chart, pH color	1	6	E/6
Clock, wind-up	1		E/3, F/4
Clock, with second hand	1		F/1
Collecting net (optional)	1		B/2
Cloth, cotton, 18" x 22"	1	1	D/3
Compass	1	6	E/7
Container, clear, w/drilled hole	1	6	D/4
Container, plastic clear, 2 qt	1	6	B/3
Container, plastic, with lid	3		B/5
Cube-O-Grams		100	C/2
Cup, graduated plastic clear, 10 oz	2	6	E/3, 4
Dropper	5	18	A/1, 4, 6; B/5; E/5
Fishbowl, 1 gal	2	2	B/1
Flashlight	4	6	D/1; F/7, 8, 9
Forceps	7	6	A/4, 6
Goggles	5		B/5, C/1, 3, 5; D/2, E/4, 5, 6; F/2, 3, 4, 9
Hand lens	12	6	A/1, A/2, 4, 5, 6; C/3, 4, 5; E/4; F/8
Hook, screw, small brass	2	12	F/2
Jar, plastic, wide-mouthed, tall, 12 oz, w/lid	6	6	C/7
Light socket, mini, w/Fahnestock Clips	2	6	E/7
Light socket, porcelain	4	6	B/3; D/1, 7; E/3
Magnet	1	6	E/4
Marbles		80	E/2
Materials, hard and soft; such as book, wood block, cloth, metal sheet, sponge, towel			F/6
Microscope	1	3	A/1, 4, 5; B/5
Microscope slide	7	72	A/1, 4, 5; B/5

Materials	Quantity Needed per group	Kit Quantity	Unit/Lesson
Mineral collection		7 specimens/ 6 each	C/3
Mirror, plastic	1	6	F/7
Meterstick	4		B/4; C/1; F/2, 6, 10
Mug	1		D/3
Object, small, to put inside box	1		F/7
Nails		15	C/3, E/5
Pail	4	6	E/1, 3
Pan, aluminum, 8" x 8" x $\frac{1}{4}$"	2	12	D/7
Pan, aluminum, 13" x 10" x 2"	3	12	C/6
Pan, aluminum, 31 cm x 22 cm x 3 cm	1	6	A/9, F/10
Paper clips	20	200	F/10
Paper clips, jumbo		300	E/1, 2
Peanuts, foam packaging		200	C/6
Petri dish	2	6	A/7, C/6
Plastic, red, blue, green, yellow, 3" x 3" sheets	1 of each	6 of each	F/9
Rock samples		14 specimens/ 6 each	C/4, 5
Ruler	4		B/1, D/1, E/1,
Ruler, metric	4		C/4, 5, 7; D/1;
Stopwatch	2	6	D/1, F10
Streak plate	2	8	C/3, 4
Strip, metal	1	6	F/1
Thermometer	7	18	D/1, 2, 3, 7; E
Thumbtack	1	100	C/7
Tornado Tube	1	6	D/6
Washers	3	18	F/1
Whisk	1	3	E/4
Wire, copper, 16 gauge		20 in.	C/4
Wire, copper, 22 gauge, plastic coated		100 ft	E/7
Wire, copper, 24 gauge, enamel coated		4 oz	E/7
Wood, block, 3" x 4" x $\frac{3}{4}$"	2	12	F/2

Consultants

LIFE SCIENCES

Dr. Carol Baskin
University of Kentucky, Lexington, KY

Dr . Joe W. Crim
University of Georgia, Athens, GA

Dr. Marie DiBerardino
Allegheny University of Health Sciences
Philadelphia, PA

Dr. R. E. Duhrkopf
Baylor University, Waco, TX

Dr. Dennis L. Nelson
Montana State University, Bozeman, MT

Dr. Fred Sack
Ohio State University, Columbus, OH

Dr. Martin VanDyke
Denver, CO

Dr. E. Peter Volpe
Mercer University, Macon, GA

EARTH SCIENCES

Dr. Clarke Alexander
Skidaway Institute of Oceanography,
Savannah, GA

Dr. Suellen Cabe
Pembroke State University, Pembroke, NC

Dr. Thomas A. Davies
Texas A & M University, College Station, TX

Dr. Ed Geary
Geological Society of America, Boulder, CO

Dr. David C.Kopaska-Merkel
Geological Survey of Alabama, Tuscaloosa, AL

PHYSICAL SCIENCES

Dr. Bonnie Buratti
Jet Propulsion Lab, Pasadena, CA

Dr. Shawn Carlson
Society of Amateur Scientists, San Diego, CA

Dr. Karen Kwitter
Williams College, Williamstown, MA

Dr. Steven Souza,
Williamstown, MA

Dr. Joseph P. Straley
University of Kentucky, Lexington, KY

Dr. Thomas Troland
University of Kentucky , Lexington, KY

Dr. Josephine Davis Wallace
University of North Carolina, Charlotte, NC

CONSULTANT FOR PRIMARY GRADES
Donna Harrell Lubcker
East Texas Baptist University, Marshall, TX

• TEACHER PANELISTS

Newark, NJ
First Avenue School
Jorge Alameda
Concetta Cioci
Neva Galasso
Bernadette Kazanjian - reviewer
Janet Mayer - reviewer
Toby Marks
Maria Tutela

Brooklyn, NY
P.S. 31
Paige McGlone
Janet Mantel
Madeline Pappas
Maria Puma - reviewer

P.S. 217
Rosemary Ahern
Charles Brown
Claudia Deeb - reviewer
Wendy Lerner

P.S. 225
Christine Calafiore
Annette Fisher - reviewer

P.S. 250
Melissa Kane

P.S. 277
Erica Cohen
Helena Conti
Anne Marie Corrado
Deborah Scott-DiClemente
Jeanne Fish
Diane Fromhartz
Tricia Hinz
Lisa Iside
Susan Malament
Joyce Menkes-reviewer
Elaine Noto
Jean Pennacchio

Jeffrey Hampton
Mwaka Yavana

Elmont, NY
Covert Avenue School
Arlene Connelly

Mt. Vernon, NY
Holmes School
Jennifer Cavallaro
Lou Ciofi
George DiFiore
Brenda Durante
Jennifer Hawkins - reviewer
Michelle Mazzotta
Catherine Moringiello
Mary Jane Oria - reviewer
Lucille Pierotti
Pia Vicario - reviewer

Ozone Park, NY
St. Elizabeth School
Joanne Cocchiola - Reviewer
Helen DiPietra - Reviewer
Barbara Kingston
Madeline Visco

St. Albans, NY
Orvia Williams

• TEACHER REVIEWERS

Peoria, IL
Rolling Acres Middle School
Gail Truho

Rockford, IL
Rockford Public Schools
Dr. Sharon Wynstra
Science Coordinator

Newark, NJ
Alexander Street School
Cheryl Simeonidis

Albuquerque, NM
Jackie Costales
Science Coordinator,
Montgomery Complex

Poughkeepsie, NY
St. Peter's School
Monica Crolius

Columbus, OH
St. Mary's School
Linda Cotter
Joby Easley

Keizer, OR
Cummings Elementary
Deanna Havel

McMinnville, OR
McMinnville School District
Kristin Ward

Salem, OR
Fruitland Elementary
Mike Knudson

Four Corners Elementary
Bethany Ayers
Sivhong Hanson
Cheryl Kirkelie
Julie Wells

Salem-Keizer Public Schools
Rachael Harms
Sue Smith,
Science Specialist

Yoshikai Elementary
Joyce Davenport

Norristown, PA
St. Teresa of Avila
Fran Fiordimondo

Pittsburgh, PA
Chartiers Valley
Intermediate School
Rosemary Hutter

Memphis, TN
Memphis City Schools
Quincy Hathorn
District Science Facilitator

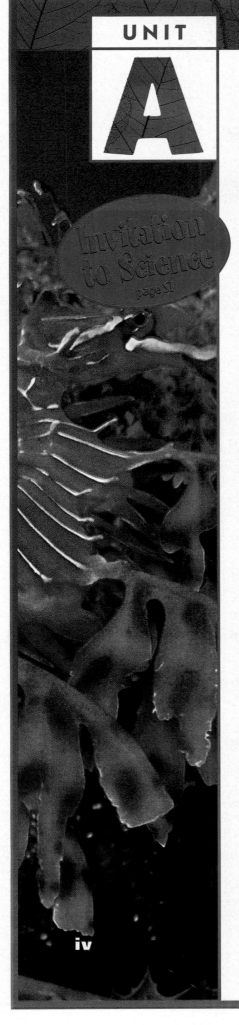

iv

Life Science

Interactions of Living Things PAGE B1

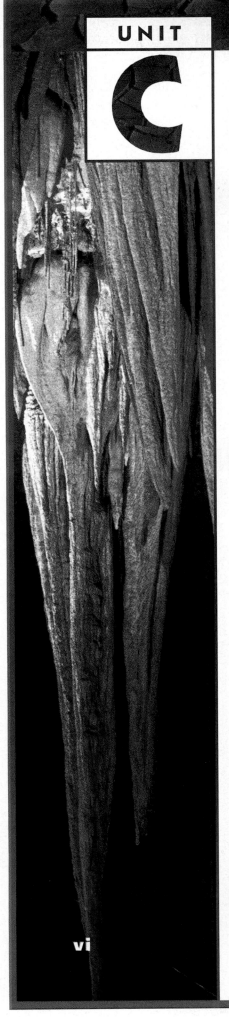

UNIT D

Earth Science

Weather and Climate PAGE D1

Physical Science
Properties of Matter and Energy PAGE E1

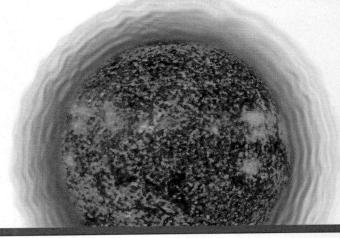

Activities

UNIT D

UNIT E

UNIT F

As you study science, you will learn many new words. You will read about many new ideas. Read these pages. They will help you understand this book.

1. The Vocabulary list has all the new words you will learn in the lesson. The page numbers tell you where the words are taught.

2. The name tells you what the lesson is about.

3. Get Ready uses the picture on the page to help you start thinking about the lesson.

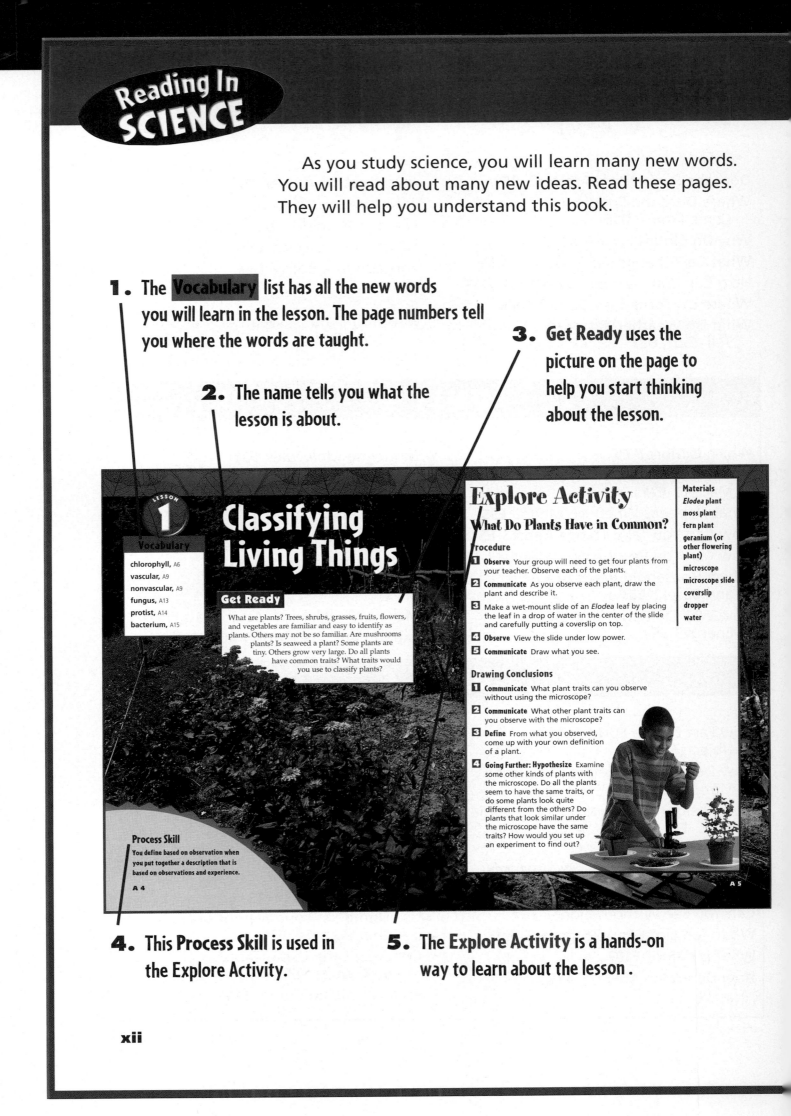

LESSON 1

Classifying Living Things

Vocabulary

chlorophyll, A6
vascular, A9
nonvascular, A9
fungus, A13
protist, A14
bacterium, A15

Get Ready

What are plants? Trees, shrubs, grasses, fruits, flowers, and vegetables are familiar and easy to identify as plants. Others may not be so familiar. Are mushrooms plants? Is seaweed a plant? Some plants are tiny. Others grow very large. Do all plants have common traits? What traits would you use to classify plants?

Process Skill

You define based on observation when you put together a description that is based on observations and experience.

A 4

Explore Activity

What Do Plants Have in Common?

Procedure

1 **Observe** Your group will need to get four plants from your teacher. Observe each of the plants.

2 **Communicate** As you observe each plant, draw the plant and describe it.

3 Make a wet-mount slide of an *Elodea* leaf by placing the leaf in a drop of water in the center of the slide and carefully putting a coverslip on top.

4 **Observe** View the slide under low power.

5 **Communicate** Draw what you see.

Drawing Conclusions

1 **Communicate** What plant traits can you observe without using the microscope?

2 **Communicate** What other plant traits can you observe with the microscope?

3 **Define** From what you observed, come up with your own definition of a plant.

4 **Going Further: Hypothesize** Examine some other kinds of plants with the microscope. Do all the plants seem to have the same traits, or do some plants look quite different from the others? Do plants that look similar under the microscope have the same traits? How would you set up an experiment to find out?

Materials

Elodea plant
moss plant
fern plant
geranium (or other flowering plant)
microscope
microscope slide
coverslip
dropper
water

A 5

4. This **Process Skill** is used in the Explore Activity.

5. The **Explore Activity** is a hands-on way to learn about the lesson .

As you read a lesson, follow these three steps. They will help you to understand what you are reading.

1. This box contains the **Main Idea** of the lesson. Keep the main idea of the lesson in mind as you read.

2. Before Reading Read the large red question before you read the page. Try to answer this question from what you already know.

3. During Reading Look for new **Vocabulary** words in yellow. Look at the pictures. They will help you understand what you are reading.

Read to Learn

Main Idea Plants make food and produce oxygen through photosynthesis.

Photosynthesis

Carbon dioxide + Water → Light, Chlorophyll → Sugar + Oxygen

What Is Photosynthesis?

When you walk to a grocery store to buy food, you are really doing two things. You are using energy to get to the store, and you are buying energy at the store. Walking uses energy. Food provides you with energy.

All living things need energy to survive. Where do they get energy? Animals eat food to get energy. Plants make their own food. However, the very process of making food uses up energy. Where does the plant get this energy? It comes from light, especially sunlight.

Light is a form of energy that plants use to make their food. Plants capture the energy of light and trap it in the foods they make. Later, when they need this energy, they get it back from the food. The food-making process is called photosynthesis (foh-tuh-SIN-thuh-sis). This term comes from Greek words that mean "putting together by light." The process is very complex, but basically here's how it happens.

First, sunlight strikes a green part of a plant, such as a leaf. The leaf is green because it has a green chemical called chlorophyll. Chlorophyll helps the plant make its food. The chlorophyll is found in plant parts called chloroplasts. The chloroplasts act like tiny chemical factories. Inside them water and carbon

Light — Cells with chlorophyll — Carbon dioxide — Sugars — Water — Oxygen

Photosynthesis Hydrogen (from water) and carbon dioxide join in the presence of sunlight and chlorophyll to form sugars and oxygen.

The water and carbon dioxide that form are released into the air.

dioxide from the air combine to make sugar and oxygen. However, this reaction could not happen without the help of light energy.

The sugars that the Sun's energy helps the leaf to make then go into the leaf's veins and off to all parts of the plant.

The oxygen the plant makes goes into the air. All animals must breathe in oxygen to stay alive. At the same time,

they breathe out carbon dioxide, which the plants need.

Now that the Sun's energy is trapped in the sugars that the plant made, how does the plant get the energy back out? Its cells use oxygen to break apart the sugar. When the sugar breaks apart, it releases energy that the plant uses. This process is called respiration (res-puh-RAY-shuhn). This is the same process that releases energy in animals.

▷ **How is photosynthesis different from respiration?**

During photosynthesis, plants change carbon dioxide and water into sugars and oxygen. During respiration, plants and animals use oxygen to break down sugar to produce energy, water, and carbon dioxide.

The oxygen is released into the air.

The sugars that form are stored in green plants.

READING Diagrams

In what process is carbon dioxide released?

Respiration In respiration, which occurs in plants and animals, sugars and oxygen join to produce water, carbon dioxide, and energy.

A 32

A 33

---

4. After Reading ▷ This arrow points to a question. It will help you check that you understand what you have read. Try to answer the question before you go to the next large red question.

PRACTICE

On one page in each lesson, you will find a question that practices the Chapter Reading Skill. In any chapter you will find one of these skills:

Main idea and supporting details
The *main idea* is what the reading is about. To find the main idea:

• Answer the red question on a page.
• Look for facts that tell more about the main idea. Pictures on the page can add supporting details.

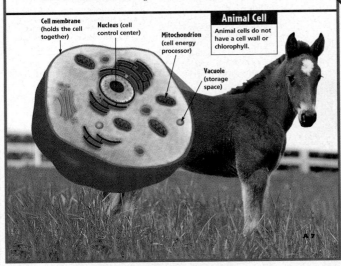

tree must be made of rigid building blocks—rigid cells that support it.

Under the microscope, *Elodea* cells look like boxes. What is one characteristic of boxes? They have walls, which keep them from collapsing into a heap. All plant cells have walls. That's why an oak tree can stand tall and strong.

The cells of all plants work together to keep the plants alive. Different kinds of cells do different kinds of jobs. Each job contributes to the health and survival of the plant. For example, in a tree, cells in leaves make the plant's food. Cells in stems, branches, roots, and the trunk form tubes through

which the food or water is moved, or *transported* (trans-PAWRT-uhd). Other cells may form flowers, fruits, and seeds that allow the tree to reproduce.

Cells are organized into *tissues* (TISH-ewz). The "strings" in celery stalks and the flesh of fruits are examples of plant tissues. Some tissues carry water and minerals to various parts of the plant. Some tissues support the plant.

READING Draw Conclusions
What is one of the things plants have in common that helps an oak tree stand tall and strong?

Cell membrane (holds the cell together)
Nucleus (cell control center)
Mitochondrion (cell energy processor)

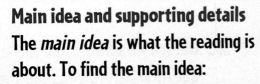

Animal Cell
Animal cells do not have a cell wall or chlorophyll.

Vacuole (storage space)

Draw conclusions
A *conclusion* is a statement of what you learned by putting the facts together. To draw a conclusion:

• Make a list of the facts you read on a page.
• Write your conclusion.

Compare and contrast *Compare* means "to tell how things are alike." *Contrast* means "to tell how things are different."

Sequence of events The *sequence* is the order in which things happen. To find the sequence:

- Ask yourself: "What happened first?" Write it down.
- Then make a list of each thing that happened after that – in order.

How Are Populations Connected?

What would happen if farmers used powerful insecticides to kill pests? What might happen if these pesticides also killed some harmless ants? Ants live in the same habitat as Texas horned lizards. Because the lizards eat ants, changes in the ant population may tell a lot about the future of the lizards.

In the food chain, the relationship doesn't stop there. Birds of prey, such as hawks, feed on the lizards. What happens to the ants will also affect the lives of these birds. A change in one population affects all the other organisms in that food chain.

Animals may adapt to changes in their habitats. A varied diet can be useful. Texas horned lizards eat mainly ants. They also eat other insects such as grasshoppers. If

the ant population decreases, the lizards can feed on grasshoppers instead. This changes the number of grasshoppers in a community, however. The other organisms that eat grasshoppers will be affected, too. A change in the ant population affects more than just a food chain. It affects all of the organisms in a food web.

Food chains and food webs help scientists predict how communities will be affected by change.

Lubber grasshoppers

Ant

Horned lizard

READING Sequence of Events How does a change in a food web affect other populations?

How Do Populations Adapt to Competition for Food?

Food webs show that animals compete for food. Fish and gulls must compete for a dinner of prawns, for example. In order to survive, an organism must adapt to competition. Sometimes this competition causes a population to change its habitat. This is what happened to Florida's green anole.

At one time green anoles could be spotted all over Florida, perched on the trunks of trees and the branches of bushes. Then a new and bigger species of anole arrived in Florida from the island of Cuba. Scientists don't know how it made the 144 km (90 mi) trip. Its size and, perhaps, other characteristics gave it a hunting edge over the small green anole, however.

Soon the smaller green anole seemed to disappear. Was it really gone? No. Scientists found the little green anole high in the trees. It had found a new habitat where it did not have to compete with the Cuban anole for food.

▶ How did the green anole adapt to competition?

The green anole (left), a native of the U.S. southeast, acquired a new habitat when Cuban anoles (above) were introduced.

B 22

B 23

Cause and effect When you read about something that happened, ask yourself: "What made it happen?"

- A *cause* makes something happen. Beating a drum is a cause.
- The thing that happens is the *effect*. The effect is the sound.

Summarize To summarize:

- Ask yourself what the page you read is about.
- State it in your own words in a sentence or two.

Reading In SCIENCE GRAPHICS

Throughout all chapters of this book, you will get information by reading graphics. Graphics are pictures that are drawn to show information.

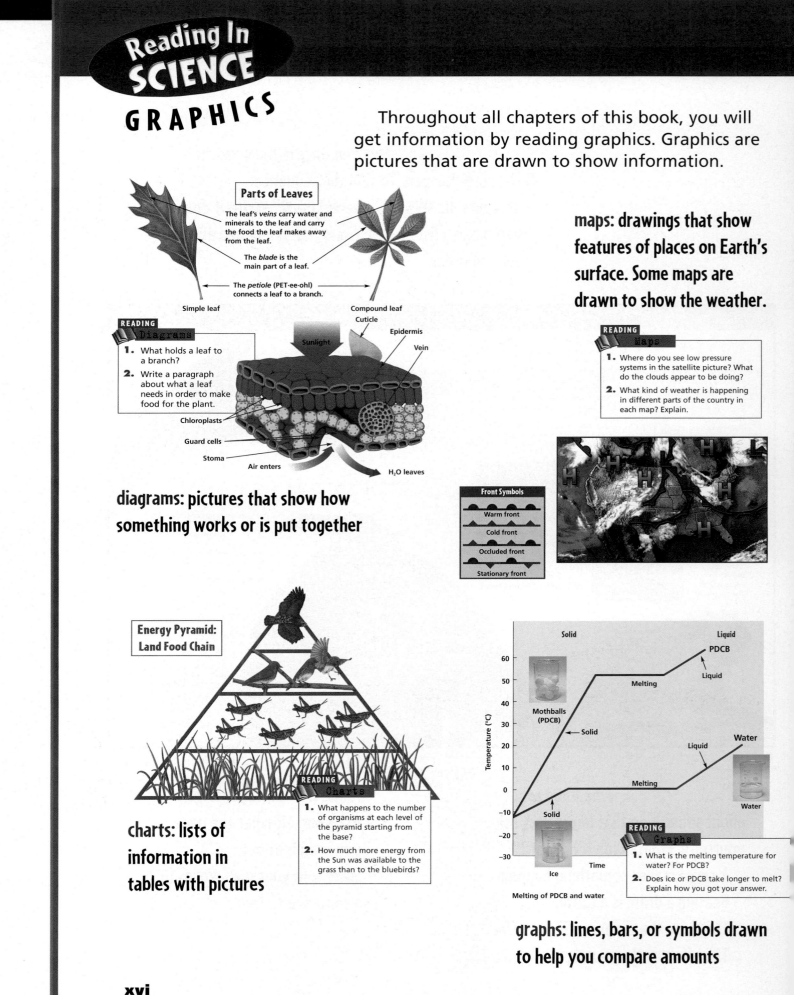

maps: drawings that show features of places on Earth's surface. Some maps are drawn to show the weather.

READING Maps
1. Where do you see low pressure systems in the satellite picture? What do the clouds appear to be doing?
2. What kind of weather is happening in different parts of the country in each map? Explain.

Parts of Leaves
The leaf's *veins* carry water and minerals to the leaf and carry the food the leaf makes away from the leaf.
The *blade* is the main part of a leaf.
The *petiole* (PET·ee·ohl) connects a leaf to a branch.
Simple leaf
Compound leaf

READING Diagrams
1. What holds a leaf to a branch?
2. Write a paragraph about what a leaf needs in order to make food for the plant.

Cuticle, Epidermis, Vein, Sunlight, Chloroplasts, Guard cells, Stoma, Air enters, H₂O leaves

diagrams: pictures that show how something works or is put together

Front Symbols
Warm front
Cold front
Occluded front
Stationary front

Energy Pyramid: Land Food Chain

READING Charts
1. What happens to the number of organisms at each level of the pyramid starting from the base?
2. How much more energy from the Sun was available to the grass than to the bluebirds?

charts: lists of information in tables with pictures

READING Graphs
1. What is the melting temperature for water? For PDCB?
2. Does ice or PDCB take longer to melt? Explain how you got your answer.

Melting of PDCB and water

graphs: lines, bars, or symbols drawn to help you compare amounts

xvi

Invitation to Science

- learn about the process science skills used throughout this book

- find out how a real-life scientist uses these skills to solve problems

Grade 3
Shirley Mah Kooyman, botanist

Grade 4
Eugenie Clarke, marine biologist

Grade 5
Walter Alvarez, geologist

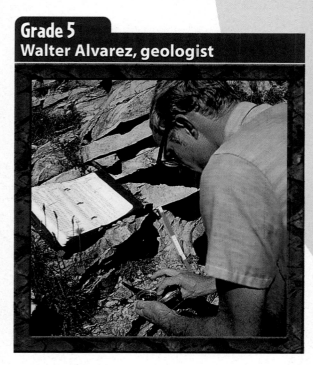

Grade 6
Neil deGrasse Tyson, astrophysicist

Invitation to Science

There are many kinds of scientists. You can be one, too.

A Scientist:

- Observes
- Infers
- Classifies
- Measures
- Uses numbers
- Communicates
- Predicts
- Interprets data
- Forms hypotheses
- Uses variables
- Experiments
- Makes models
- Defines terms based on observations

Science Process Skills

Observe to use one or more of the senses to identify or learn about an object or event

Infer to form an idea from facts or observations

Classify to place things that share properties together in groups

Measure to find the size, distance, time, volume, area, mass, weight, or temperature of an object or event

Use numbers to order, count, add, subtract, multiply, and divide to explain data

Communicate to share information

Predict to state possible results of an event or experiment

Interpret data to use the information that has been gathered to answer questions or solve a problem

Form a hypothesis to make a statement that can be tested to answer a question

Use variables to identify things in an experiment that can be changed or controlled

Experiment to perform a test to support or disprove a hypothesis

Make a model to make something to represent an object or event

Define based on observations to put together a description that is based on observations and experience

Science Safety Tips

In the Classroom

- Read all directions. Make sure you understand them. When you see **BE CAREFUL!**, be sure to follow the safety rule.
- Listen to your teacher for special safety directions. If you don't understand something, ask for help.
- Wash your hands with soap and water before an activity.
- Wear safety goggles when your teacher tells you to wear them. Wear them when working with anything that can fly into your eyes or when working with liquids.
- Wear a safety apron if you work with anything messy or anything that might spill.
- Wipe up a spill right away or ask your teacher for help.
- Tell your teacher if something breaks. If glass breaks, do not clean it up yourself.
- Keep your hair and clothes away from open flames. Tie back long hair, and roll up long sleeves.
- Be careful around a hot plate. Know when it is on and when it is off. Remember that the plate stays hot for a few minutes after it's turned off.

- Keep your hands dry around electrical equipment.
- Don't eat or drink anything during an experiment.
- Put equipment back the way your teacher tells you.
- Dispose of things the way your teacher tells you.
- Clean up your work area after an activity and wash your hands with soap and water.

In the Field

- Go with a trusted adult—such as your teacher or a parent or guardian.
- Do not touch animals or plants without an adult's approval. The animal might bite. The plant might be poison ivy or another dangerous plant.

Responsibility

- Treat living things, the environment, and one another with respect.